Gustave Eiffel's Spectacular Idea

# The Eiffel Tower

PICTURE WINDOW BOOKS
a capstone imprint

by Sharon Katz Cooper

illustrated by Janna Bock

The people of France needed to plan a party—a huge party. In five years their country would be hosting the 1889 World's Fair. People would be coming from around the world to show off their latest inventions, artwork, and products. The Fair had to be amazing.

The French government held a contest to design a centerpiece for the Fair. Gustave Eiffel couldn't wait to enter. He knew he had a winning idea. A spectacular idea! An idea that would make everyone in France proud.

By the time of the contest in 1884, Gustave was already a famous engineer. He had built many railroad bridges and viaducts. He had built the world's highest railway bridge. He was known for designing iron forms that could withstand strong winds.

Gustave's works stood in North America, South America, Europe, and Asia. One of his most famous works welcomed people to the United States. Gustave had designed and built the skeleton inside the Statue of Liberty!

Gustave worked hard on his contest design. He drew an iron tower that would stand 1,000 feet (305 meters) tall. It would be almost twice as tall as the brand-new Washington Monument in Washington, D.C. At 555 feet (170 m) tall, the monument was then the world's tallest building. Gustave's tower would beat it.

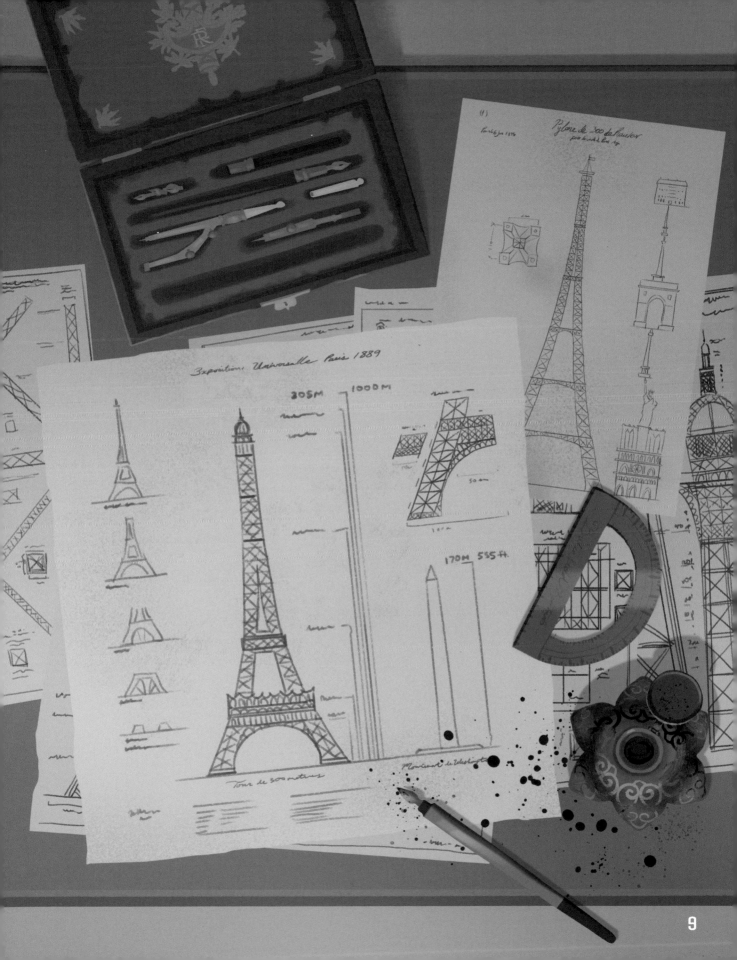

News about Gustave's tower spread throughout Paris. It became the project everyone loved to hate. Some people said the design looked "hideously unfinished." Others worried that the tower would fall over. Still others wondered how Gustave would be able to find workers. Who would want to work so high above the ground? Someone even thought the tower might turn into a giant magnet.

Yet in 1886 the government gave Gustave good news. His design had beaten 106 others. He had won the contest!

Gustave didn't know that his tower troubles were just beginning.

Gustave thought it would cost about $1 million to build the tower. The French government could pay for only one-third of that amount. Gustave needed to find the other two-thirds. To help him get investors, the government made a deal with Gustave. He could keep the tower up for 20 years and keep all the money he earned from entry fees. That money could be used to pay back investors. Gustave agreed to the deal, but months went by with no contract. Work could not begin.

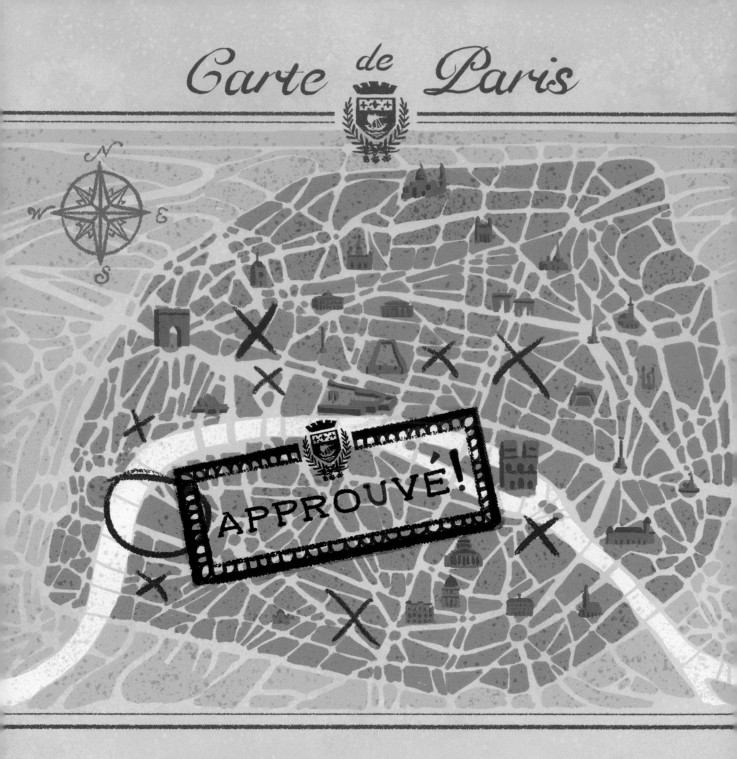

There were a lot of questions about where to build the giant tower. Gustave looked at many sites. Finally, in November 1886, he found the perfect spot. The government agreed to a contract. "I can get started at last," Gustave said.

But wait! Two women who lived close to the building site filed a lawsuit to stop Gustave. They did not want to live in the tower's shadow. They were afraid Gustave's tower might fall down on them.

Gustave was nervous. If he did not start soon, the tower wouldn't be finished in time for the World's Fair. Gustave told the government he would take care of the lawsuit on his own. On January 7, 1887, the contract was signed.

Construction began on January 26, and the race was on. Workers had little more than two years to build the giant tower. They started by digging holes for the tower's feet.

Even after construction began, people complained. "Your tower is horrible and ugly," some said. A group of famous people tried to stop construction. They wrote, "This is the horror the French have found to give us an idea of the taste they boast about?"

But Gustave was not bothered. He said people loved grand things. Look at the pyramids of Egypt! "I believe that the tower will have its own beauty," he said. "Why would what is admirable in Egypt become hideous and ridiculous in Paris?"

Travel to
EGYPT

Workers dug for five months. Then they started putting together the pillars. More than 18,000 parts would be used to build the entire tower.

By the end of 1887, workers reached the first platform. They finished it the following April. Gustave soon opened a workers' lunchroom there. Men could now take lunch breaks on the tower instead of going all the way down to the ground.

The tower grew. By July 1888 it stood more than 330 feet (100 m) tall. Work began on the second platform. It seemed things were going well.

But in the fall, workers went on strike. They wanted a raise. Gustave knew time was running out, so he agreed. He also gave the workers warm, waterproof clothes for the winter ahead. By the end of 1888, the tower was taller than the Washington Monument.

Workers put in many long hours. The people of Paris watched as the tower grew to its full height of 984 feet (300 m).

The last big piece of the project was an elevator system. Elevators were still fairly new at the time. Gustave wasn't sure if they would work in his tower. But they did. After a few finishing touches, including paint and lights, the Eiffel Tower was ready.

On March 31, 1889, Gustave and a few important guests climbed the tower's 1,710 steps for the first time. There they raised a huge French flag. "The French flag," Gustave later wrote, "is the only one with a 300-meter [984-foot] pole."

The Eiffel Tower opened to visitors on May 15, 1889. It had taken two years, two months, and five days to complete. Gustave needed his tower to be a hit—and it was! During the Fair's six months, nearly 2 million people visited the Eiffel Tower—nearly 12,000 people each day. Gustave's idea became the jewel of Paris.

# Afterword

After the Fair was over, Gustave found many uses for his tower. He and his scientist friends used the tower to study wind and weather. Later they used the tower as a giant radio antenna. Gustave even had a small lab on the third platform.

The Eiffel Tower did not come down after 20 years, as planned. It became—and remains to this day—the symbol of Paris. It is one of the most famous structures in the world. It took 40 years before another building—the Chrysler Building in New York—passed its height. Today 6 million visitors go up the Eiffel Tower each year.

Gustave Eiffel died in 1923 at age 91.

Gustave Eiffel, circa 1889

Eiffel Tower

# Glossary

**admirable**—liked and respected

**antenna**—a wire or dish that sends or receives radio waves

**boast**—to brag

**centerpiece**—the main focus or attraction

**contract**—a legal agreement to do something

**engineer**—a person who designs and builds machines

**investor**—someone who provides money for a project in return for a share in the profits

**lawsuit**—a legal case begun in a court by one person who claims something from another

**platform**—a raised, flat surface

**spectacular**—very exciting; breathtaking

**strike**—when someone stops doing his or her job because of a disagreement over pay or working conditions

**symbol**—a design or object that stands for something else

# Critical Thinking Using the Common Core

1. Why was Gustave the perfect man to design and build a very tall iron tower? **[Integration of Knowledge and Ideas]**

2. Name the problems Gustave ran into while trying to build his iron tower. Then describe how he solved each of them. **[Key Ideas and Details]**

3. How was the Eiffel Tower paid for? **[Key Ideas and Details]**

# Read More

Colson, Mary. *France.* Countries Around the World. Chicago: Heinemann Library, 2012.

LaPlante, Walter. *The Statue of Liberty.* Symbols of America. New York: Gareth Stevens Publishing, 2015.

Wilbur, Helen L. *E Is for Eiffel Tower: A France Alphabet.* Ann Arbor, Mich.: Sleeping Bear Press, 2010.

# Internet Sites

FactHound offers a safe, fun way to find Internet sites related to this book. All of the sites on FactHound have been researched by our staff.

Here's all you do:

Visit *www.facthound.com*

Type in this code: 9781479571369

Check out projects, games and lots more at
**www.capstonekids.com**

# Look for all the books in the series:

 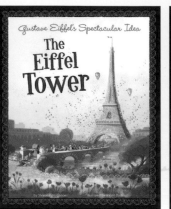 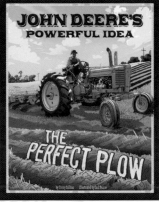 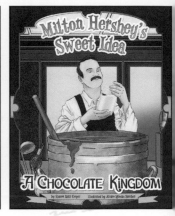

Special thanks to our adviser for his expertise:
Terry Flaherty, PhD, Professor of English
Minnesota State University, Mankato

Editor: Jill Kalz
Designer: Lori Bye
Creative Director: Nathan Gassman
Production Specialist: Laura Manthe
The illustrations in this book were created digitally.

Picture Window Books are published by Capstone,
1710 Roe Crest Drive, North Mankato, Minnesota 56003
www.capstonepub.com

Getty Images/Mondadori Portfolio, 29 (right); Shutterstock/
majeczka, 29 (left)

Library of Congress Cataloging-in-Publication Data
Cataloging-in-publication information is on file with the Library
of Congress.
ISBN 978-1-4795-7136-9 (library binding)
ISBN 978-1-4795-7166-6 (paperback)
ISBN 978-1-4795-7178-9 (eBook PDF)

Printed in the United States of America in
North Mankato, Minnesota.
062019    000084